To make a vivid moving optical illusion, you need two things: a certain type of pattern and a plastic overlay. Simply sliding the overlay across the pattern brings it to life.

In this book, Tim Armstrong shows how to make patterns which vibrate or rotate or pulsate or jiggle or wobble or dance or…, well try some and see!

Tim Armstrong developec
Slade School of Art 1967–
at the Royal Academy S
"British Movements '69" ;
the exhibition of British
Bromsgrove, Birminghan

From 1969—78 he lectl
Exhibitions included the E
touring exhibition "Eleve
Plains Art Museum and '
Minnesota. In 1977, the
him to paint two murals, e
Ends Scheme in Glasgo\

His works are in many p
now teaches at the Cam

Make Moving Patterns
How to create your own optical illusions
© Tim Armstrong 1982
ISBN 0 906212 26 X
Design Elizabeth Chesworth
Printed by Ancient House Press, Ipswich

Straubruke
Diss
Norfolk IP21 5JP

2

Contents
To make a moving pattern you need two things, a certain kind of pattern and a plastic overlay....

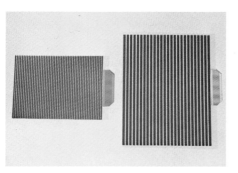

HOW TO MAKE THE OVERLAYS
Cut the plastic close to the spine and remove the overlays from the book. Keep the wall mobile overlay safely until you need it, and fix handles on to the other two. The handles are on page 27.

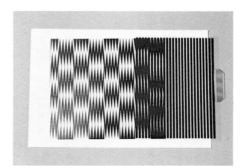

USING THE STANDARD OVERLAY
Simply slide the overlay across the page and the patterns will move. You will find that certain directions and certain speeds increase the effect and that many different kinds of movement can be achieved. Explanations and suggestions are given on pages 10 to 15.

USING THE FINE OVERLAY
This half-scale overlay animates the half-scale patterns in exactly the same way. On pages 4 to 9 Tim Armstrong demonstrates a wide variety of techniques and possibilities which, it is hoped, will serve as an inspiration for experiments of your own.

GRIDS FOR EXPERIMENT
See pages 29–58
You will find many different grids in different colours to cut out and glue down on your working paper to create new designs. All are based on the same scale and all have alignment guides printed on the back to help with accuracy. Build up your own patterns using the 'cut and glue' collage techniques, and then use the standard overlay to animate them.

THE OPTICAL ILLUSION WALL MOBILE
See pages 16–22
This model has a central 'magic window' in which a design appears to rotate like a two-way windmill as you turn your head or pass it by. Instructions for assembly are given on page 16, and the overlay is inside the front cover.

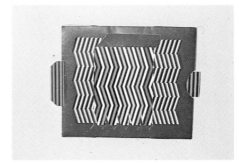

THE GENUINE SLIDING QUANTIFACT
See pages 23–28
This ingenious device allows two patterns to pass through each other, or rather four, because there are two on each side. At any stage of the intermingling, the patterns can be animated with the standard overlay. Instructions for assembly are given on page 16.

3

PATTERNS WHICH VIBRATE
Use the fine overlay

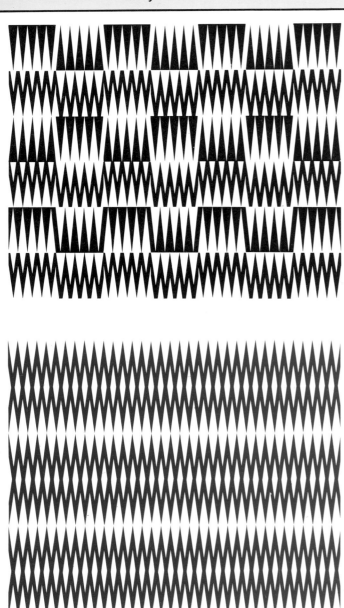

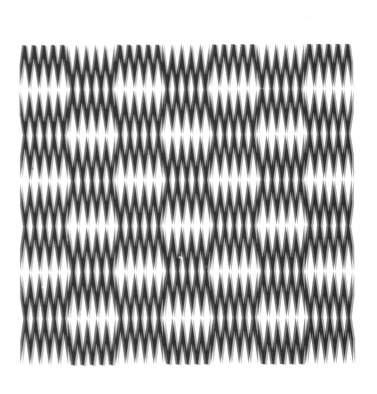

PATTERNS WHICH VIBRATE
Use the fine overlay

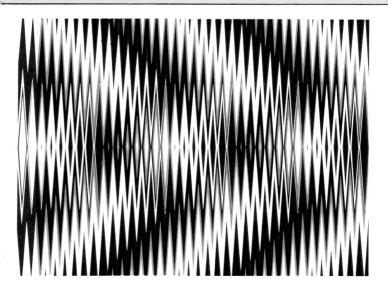

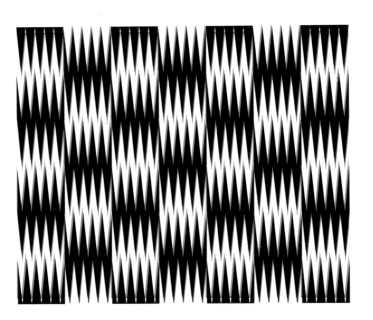

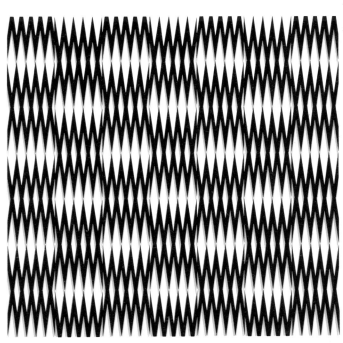

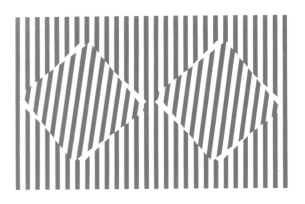

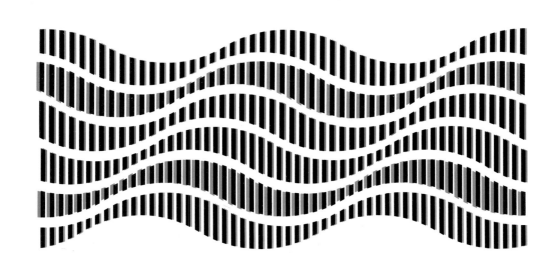

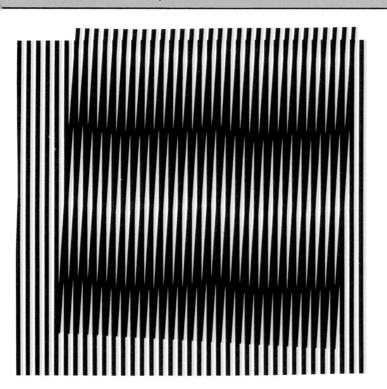

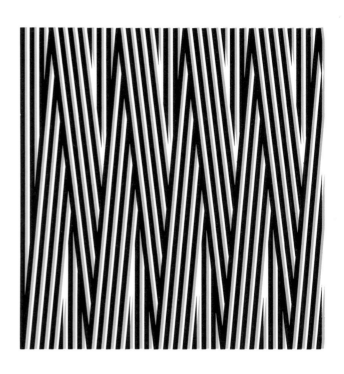

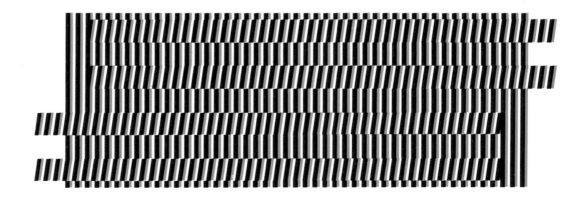

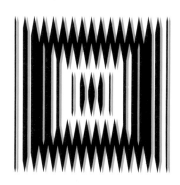

PATTERNS WHICH ROTATE
Use the fine overlay

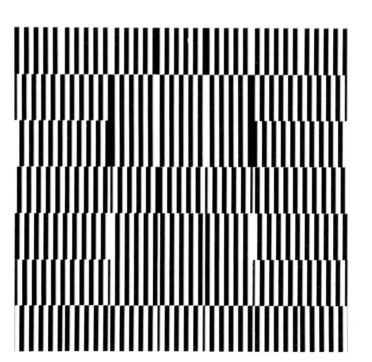

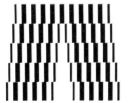

STANDARD GRIDS
Use the standard overlay

STANDARD SPACING — Switches on and off

The standard grid has exactly five lines and five spaces to the inch and is 50% line, 50% space. The standard overlay is drawn to the same scale, but is 70% line, 30% space because this combination has been found to give the most dramatic effect.

Slide the standard overlay across these two patterns. See how they switch on and off if the lines of the grid and the overlay are parallel.

Note how the two blocks of grid are out of step. One switches on as the other switches off. This is a property which can be used to introduce colour changes.

STANDARD SPACING — Switches off and on

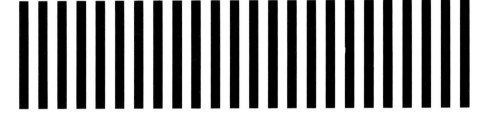

Some very attractive designs can be made with the standard grids without any complex measurement. Here are just a few ideas.

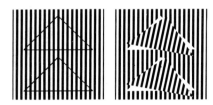

Some shapes can be cut from an area of grid, given a twist and replaced. Or work with pieces of different colours and exchange triangles.

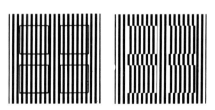

Another possibility is to replace the cut-out pieces a little to the side, but with the grid lines still parallel.

You can cut vertical strips and replace them diagonally.

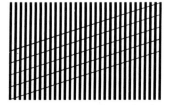

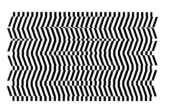

You can cut diagonal strips and replace them horizontally.

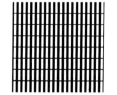

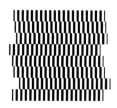

You can cut horizontal strips and then exchange with other colours, or displace them to one side.

FLOW AND COUNTERFLOW
Use the standard overlay

WIDE SPACING — Motion in the same direction as the overlay

The standard grid has here been enlarged by 5% to give slightly less than 5 lines and 5 spaces to the inch. The grid is still 50% line, 50% space. The effect is known as 'flow', where the motion is in the same direction as the motion of the overlay.

NARROW SPACING — Motion in the opposite direction to the overlay

The standard grid has here been reduced by 5% to give slightly more than five lines and five spaces to the inch, while keeping 50% line, 50% space. The effect is known as 'counterflow', where the motion is in the opposite direction to the motion of the overlay.

Strips of the standard, wide and narrow grids may be cut up and combined to give a variety of effects.

'FOUR PHASE' MOTION
Use the standard overlay

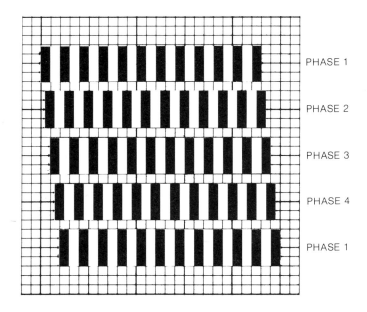

PHASE 1

PHASE 2

PHASE 3

PHASE 4

PHASE 1

Many beautiful moving patterns use the technique of 'four phase' motion. The four phases are obtained by displacing the standard grid to the right, half a line at a time.

In this diagram, strips of standard grid have been placed on a background of lines one tenth of an inch apart to show how it is done. Note that it takes four steps or phases to come back 'in phase' again. In phases 1 and 3 lines are opposite spaces and spaces are opposite lines. They are said to be 'out of phase'. Phases 2 and 4 are also 'out of phase'.

Slide the standard overlay across this diagram to see how the blocks 'switch on', one after the other.

USING THE ALIGNMENT GUIDES

The alignment guides printed on the back of each of the 'grids for experiment' are based on a unit of one tenth of an inch and so they are very useful for aligning the four phase motion. But do remember that you are looking at the back, and that phase 2 is to the left of phase 1!

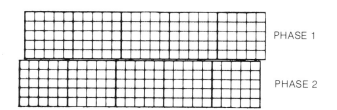

PHASE 1

PHASE 2

HOW TO MAKE A PATTERN ROTATE

If the blocks of standard grid which are arranged in four phases are set out in a cyclic way 1, 2, 3, 4, 1, 2, 3, 4, 1 ... etc., then the pattern will rotate. This pattern shows how ten blocks can be arranged to give a simple rotation — clockwise when the standard overlay is moved to the right and anticlockwise when it is moved to the left.

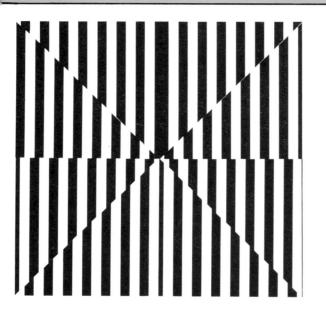

HOW TO MAKE A ROTATING SQUARE

In order to make a pattern rotate smoothly it needs to have at least two complete cycles of the four phases 1, 2, 3, 4. This square, which is divided up into eight regions is one of the simplest rotating patterns and is not difficult to make. Just follow the step by step instructions.

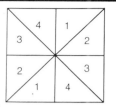

1.
Draw a square divided into 8 pieces on the alignment guide on the back of a standard grid and cut into pieces. Draw also the same diagram slightly smaller on your working paper.

2.
Glue two pieces into position so that they are in phase. This is easy to check using an overlay as a measure. Call this phase 1. Trim off the overlapping edges.

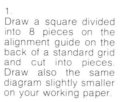

3.
Glue two more pieces into position so that they are exactly out of phase. This is phase 3. Trim the edges.

4.
Now put in the pieces for phases 2 and 4 to complete your rotating square.

HOW TO MAKE A PULSATING SQUARE

In order to make a pattern which pulsates you make use of the same four phase motion but the regions are not arranged in a cyclic way. Here the regions step inwards towards the centre. The pattern pulses inwards if you move the overlay to the right and outwards if you move it to the left.

To make a square pulsate, cut out a series of concentric squares from a single piece of standard grid. The alignment guide will help keep everything accurate.

Replace the pieces, calling the outside square phase 1. Glue the other pieces in phases 2, 3, 4, 1, . . . etc. until you get to the centre.

TRIANGULAR GRIDS
Use the standard overlay

A whole range of interesting patterns can be made, still of course based on the standard grid of ten lines to the inch but by constructing triangles instead of parallel lines inside the grid spaces.

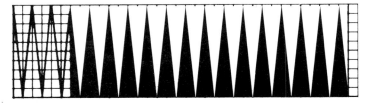

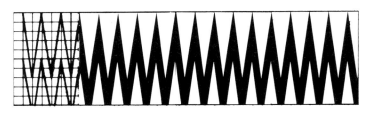

Here the sloping lines are drawn in alternate grid spaces to give five triangles to the inch. This way up they are called 'spikes' and the other way up 'icicles'. Some people might prefer to call them 'stalagmites' and 'stalactites'. The effect is a kind of vibration.

Here the spikes are made lighter or hollowed out. The effect is to give a much clearer vibration.

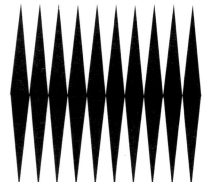

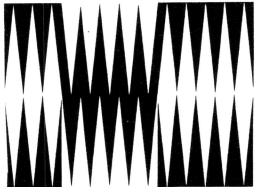

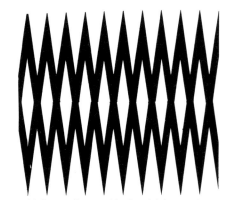

'Spikes' and 'icicles' may be combined to be 'in phase'. The effect is to give a double vibration or 'heart beat'.

Here the triangles are placed alternately and with the rows out of phase. The effect is a kind of counter-pulse. It is further developed on the grid sheets "spikes and icicles".

Hollow spikes and hollow icicles are here combined to give a clear double vibration which is very sensitive to changes of orientation of the overlay.

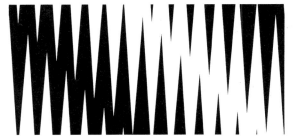

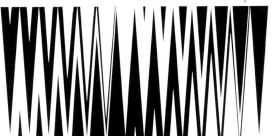

The bases of the spikes and icicles are here no longer at right angles to the grid lines, but slope downwards. It is further developed on the grid sheets called "chevrons".

This complex combination of hollow triangles is further developed on the grid sheet called "flickering arrows".

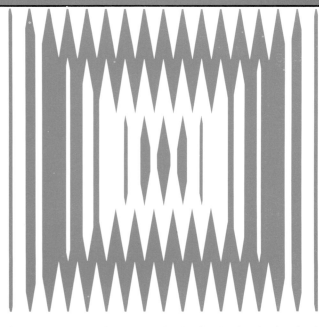

Apart from the hundreds of designs which can be created from the 'grids for experiment' pages by combining the different kinds of outline, there is another range of possibilities. You can make a background by drawing a set of parallel lines one tenth of an inch apart or purchase some suitable graph paper. Then, working on this background you can combine parallels, triangles, sloping lines, in phase and out of phase sections and so on to generate new designs at will. It will take some experiment and some experience to find combinations which are pleasing, but the finished results can be very satisfying indeed. It is always possible to combine successful pieces or eliminate unsuccessful parts by the use of 'cut and glue' collage techniques.

The design on this page was obtained in this way. Markers, coloured pencils or felt tip pens can be used to introduce colour, but a better way, if it is feasible, is to use screen printing. Once a stencil for a suitable design has been made, then it can be printed in different coloured inks, or overprinted to give colour effects similar to those used in this book.

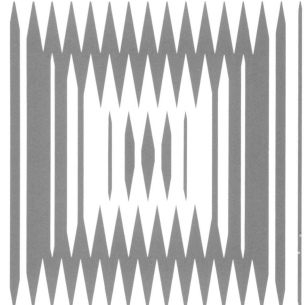

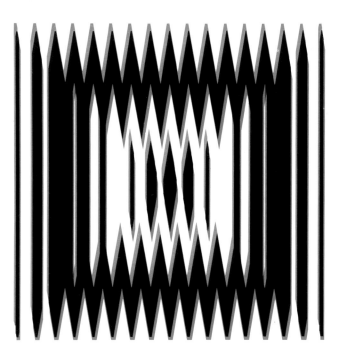

HOW TO MAKE THE OPTICAL ILLUSION WALL MOBILE

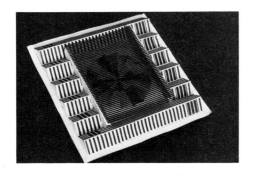

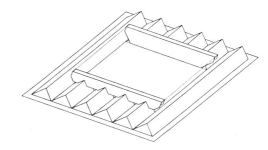

1. Cut out the seven pieces on pages 17, 19, 21. Each piece has its name on the back.

Scoring

Paper is scored so that it will fold cleanly exactly along the required lines, and so that the models will have crisp and accurate edges. The easiest way is to rule along the lines with a ball point pen which has run out of ink. Experienced model makers can use a craft knife very lightly, being careful not to cut right through the paper.

2. Score, fold towards you and crease firmly along all the lines marked ---------------to give valley folds.

3. Score, fold away from you and crease firmly along all the lines marked — — — — — to give hill folds.

4. The base is not scored. The markings _._._. _._._. simply show where the other pieces are glued.

5. Cut along the four slits marked _____ on each of the top and bottom sections.

6. Make up the top and bottom sections and glue them into position using the letters AB and CD.

7. Make up the left and right sections and glue them into position using the letters EF and GH.

8. Both overlay supports press into their corresponding slits and then glue into place using ▲ and ★ to help position them. See the diagram above.

9. Cut out the wall mobile overlay and glue into place on the supports to make the 'magic window'.

10. The wall mobile is then complete and ready for display.

HOW TO MAKE THE GENUINE SLIDING QUANTIFACT

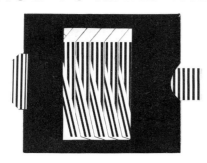

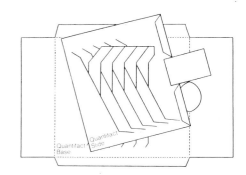

1. Cut out the six pieces on pages 23, 25 and 28. Each piece is named.

Scoring

Paper is scored so that it will fold cleanly exactly along the required lines, and so that the models will have crisp and accurate edges. The easiest way is to rule along the lines with a ball point pen which has run out of ink. Experienced model makers can use a craft knife very lightly, being careful not to cut right through the paper.

2. With a craft knife carefully cut along the solid cut lines on the base and on the slide. It is very important to cut precisely and cleanly to the exact ends of the lines.

3. Score, fold towards you and crease firmly along all the lines marked-----------to give valley folds.

4. On the left handle, fold away from you and crease firmly along the line marked — — — — — — to give a hill fold.

5. Glue down the strengthening flaps A, B, C, D.

6. Glue the right handle E into place.

7. Glue the left front and right front on to the base using flaps F and G. This completes the jacket.

8. Place the slide into the jacket and thread the fingers through the slits as in this diagram.

9. Ease the handle through its slot and fold over the flaps of the jacket. Gently check that it will slide freely, although of course it will not slide properly until the next stage is complete.

10. Spread small amounts of the glue on the areas marked H, I, J, K, L only and press the flap down firmly. When it is fastened, glue flaps M, N, O, P into position.

11. Glue the left handle into place and your quantifact is complete. The two patterns on each side should slide freely and easily through each other.

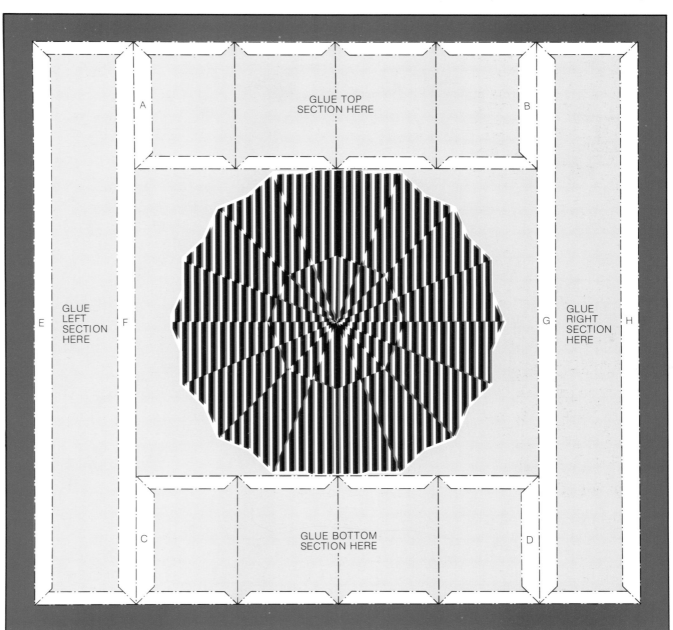

WALL MOBILE BASE

THE OPTICAL ILLUSION WALL MOBILE

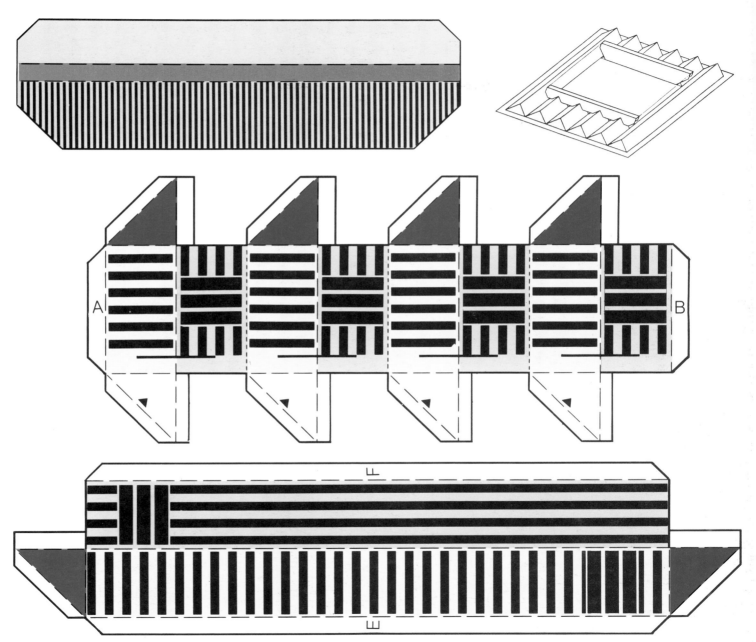

A   B

F

E

19

TOP OVERLAY SUPPORT

▲   ▲   ▲   ▲

TOP SECTION

LEFT
SECTION

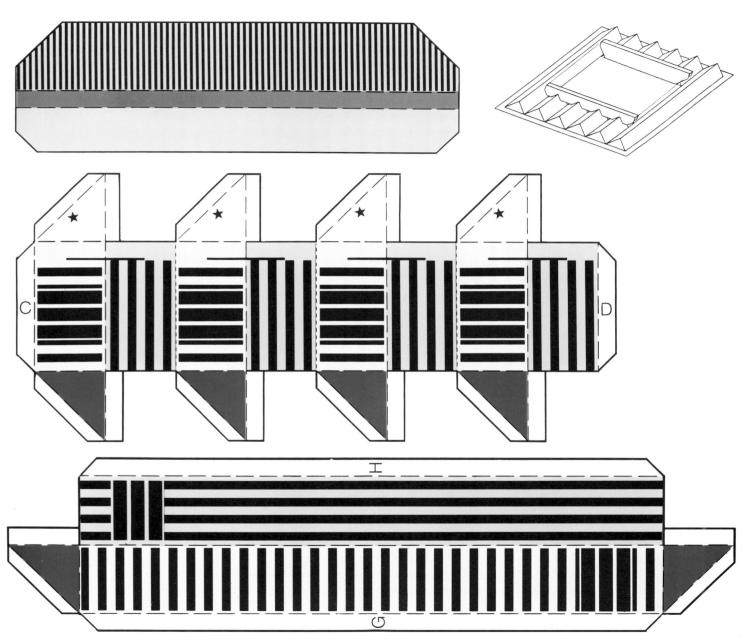

C

D

H

G

★   ★   ★   ★

BOTTOM OVERLAY SUPPORT

BOTTOM SECTION

RIGHT
SECTION

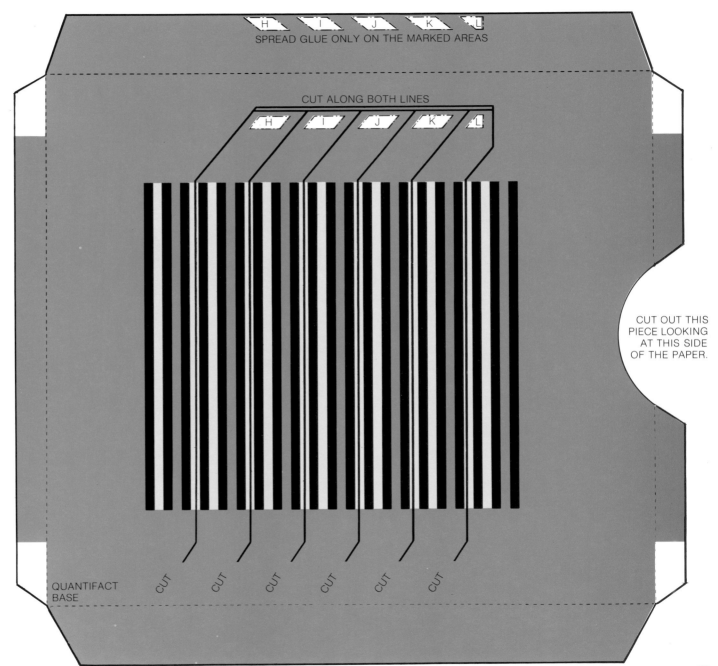

SPREAD GLUE ONLY ON THE MARKED AREAS

CUT ALONG BOTH LINES

CUT OUT THIS
PIECE LOOKING
AT THIS SIDE
OF THE PAPER.

QUANTIFACT
BASE

CUT CUT CUT CUT CUT CUT

P ▶

◀ M

▲G

▲F

▲G

O ▶

◀ N

24

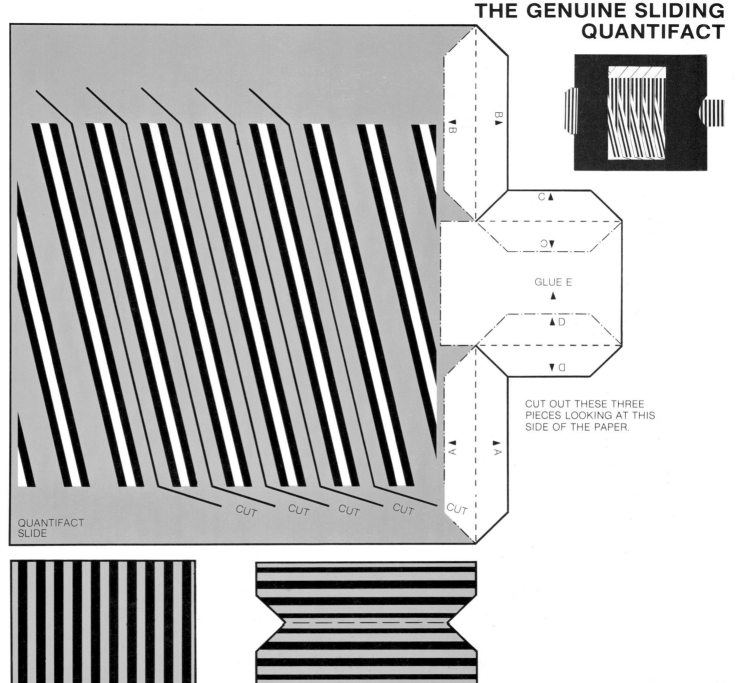

B ◀
▼ B
▲ B

C ▲
◀ C ▼

GLUE E
▲

▲ D
▼ D

CUT OUT THESE THREE
PIECES LOOKING AT THIS
SIDE OF THE PAPER.

◀ A
▲ A

CUT

QUANTIFACT
SLIDE

CUT   CUT   CUT   CUT

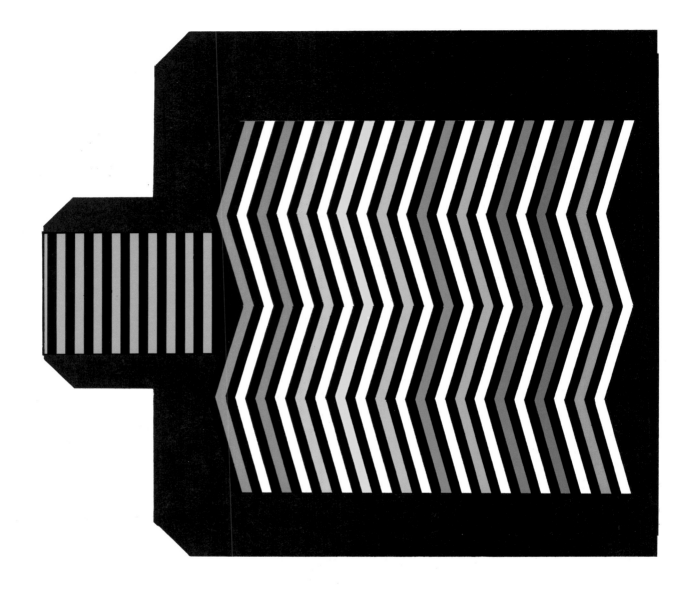

LEFT HANDLE

RIGHT HANDLE
▲
GLUE E

THE GENUINE SLIDING QUANTIFACT

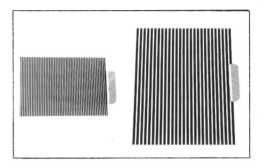

The fine overlay is bound into the book inside the front cover and the standard overlay inside the back cover. Cut along the dotted line and remove them.
To fix a handle first cut it from this page. Then score along the dotted line and fold it away from you. Spread the glue inside the fold and then grip the overlay with it. A grip of 6mm or a quarter of an inch is sufficient.

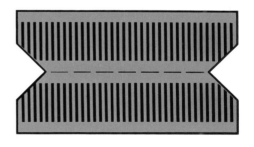

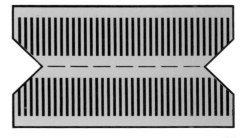

CUT OUT THESE TWO PIECES LOOKING AT
THIS SIDE OF THE PAPER.

HANDLE FOR
FINE OVERLAY

HANDLE FOR
STANDARD OVERLAY

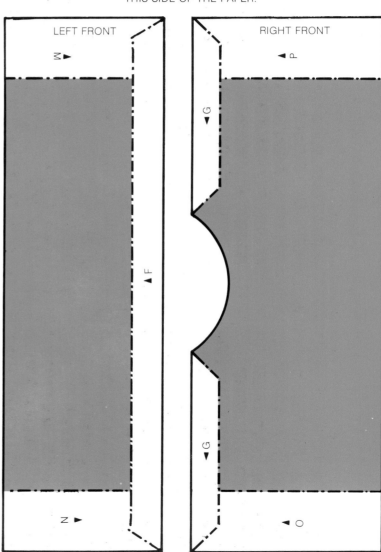

28

STANDARD SPACING

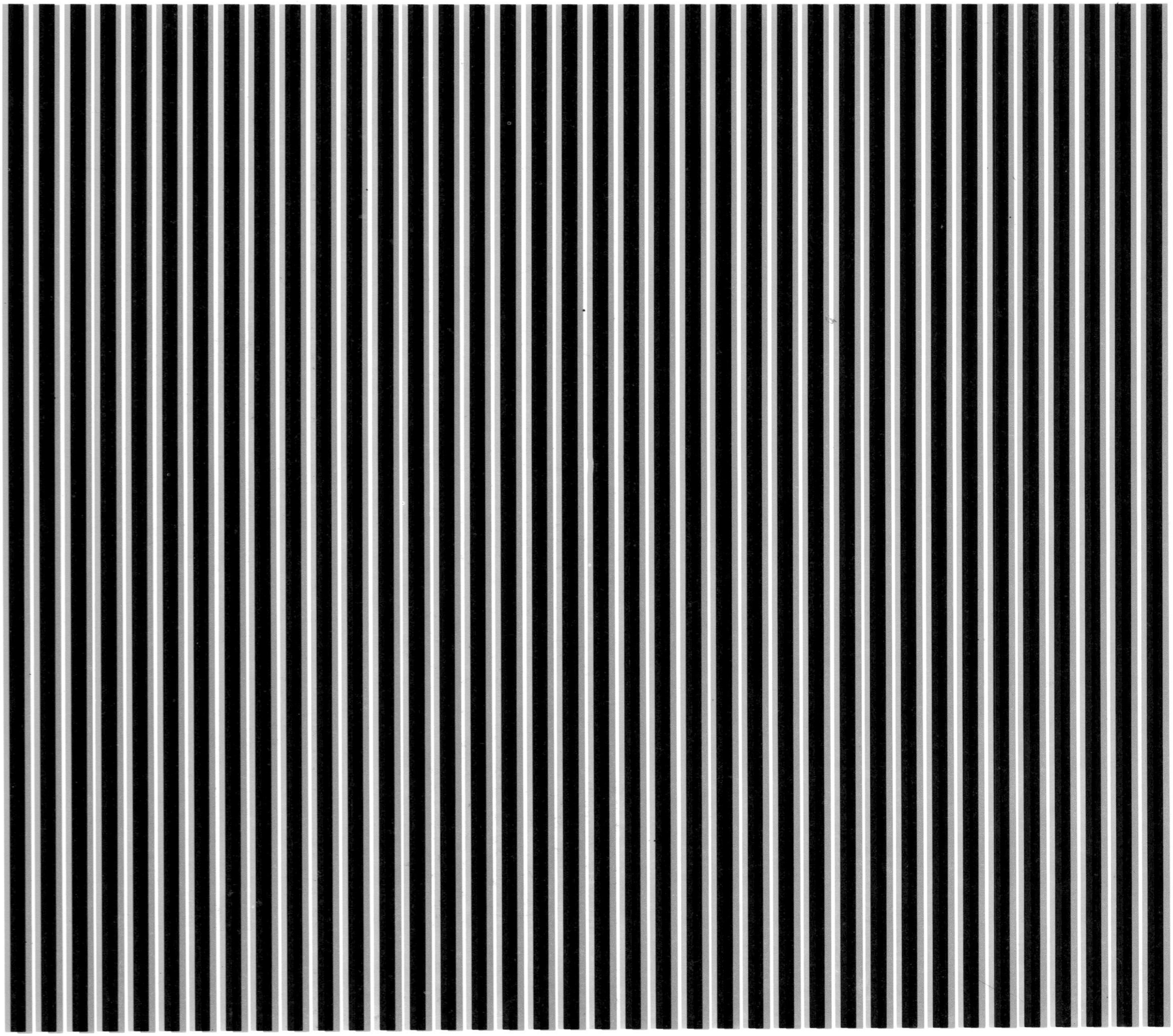

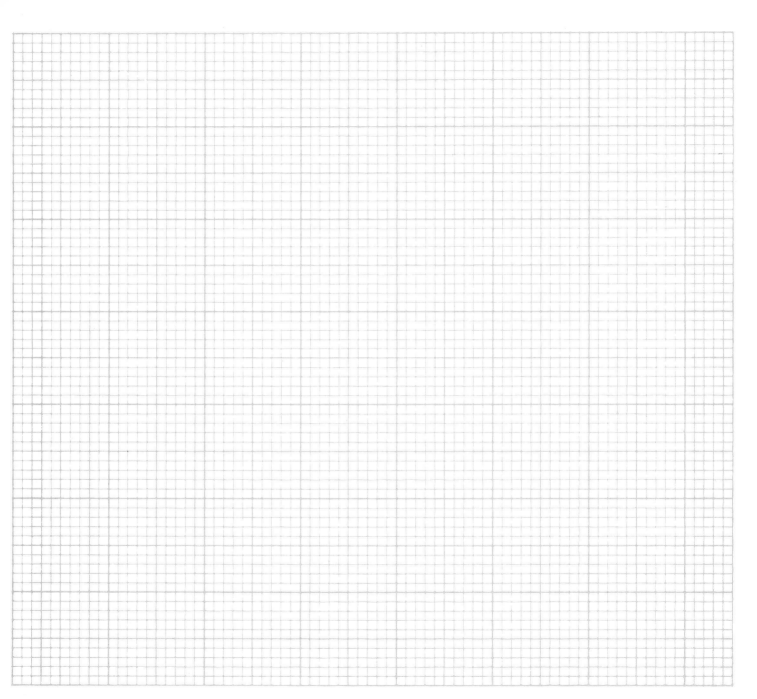

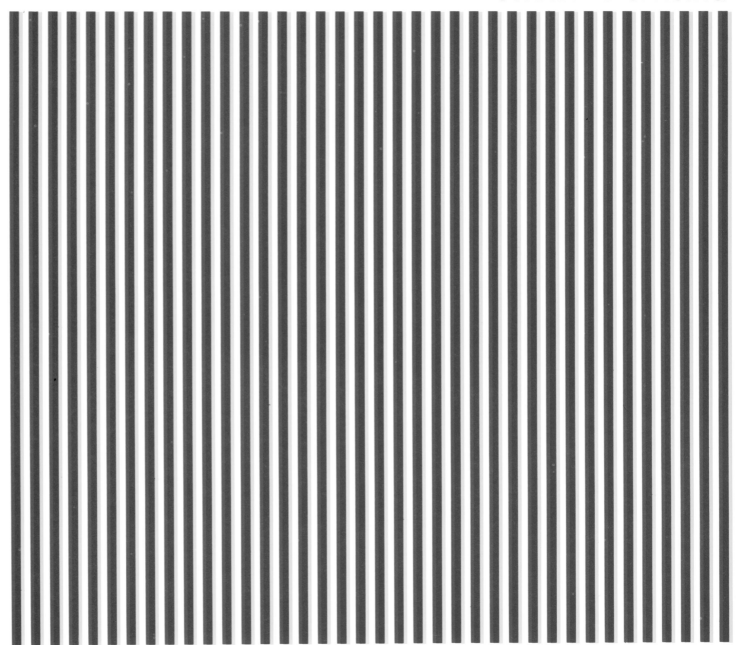

STANDARD SPACING

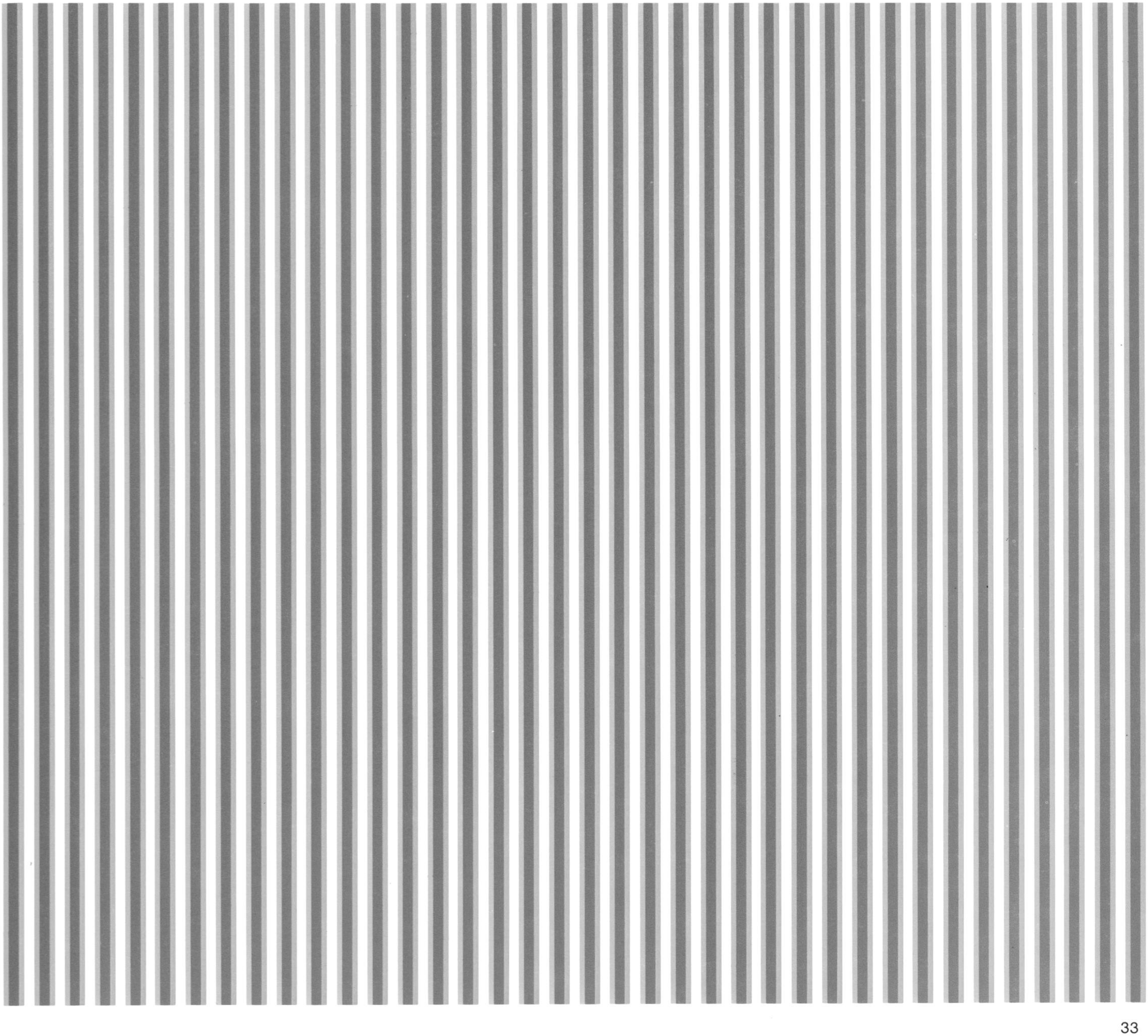

STANDARD SPACING

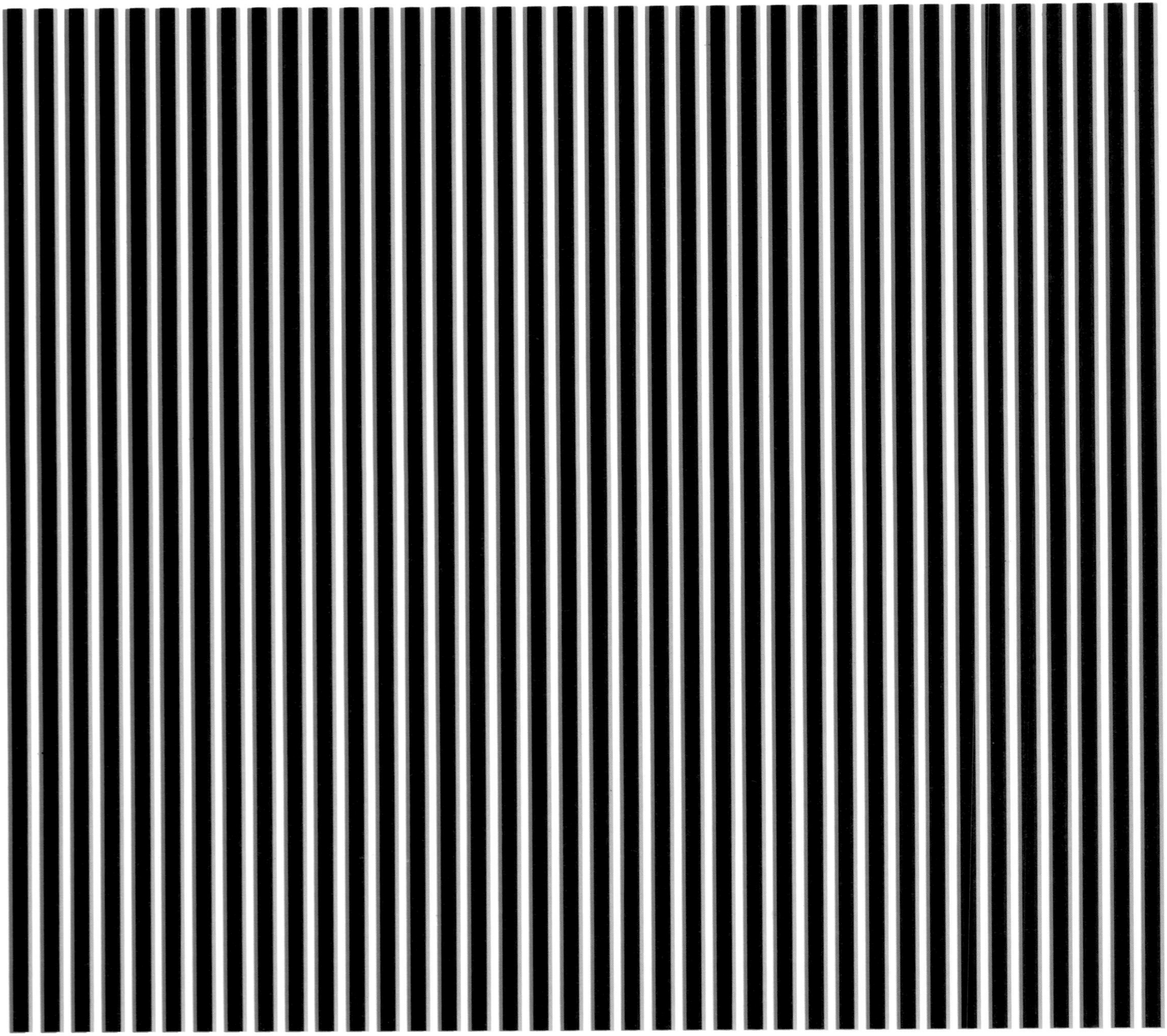

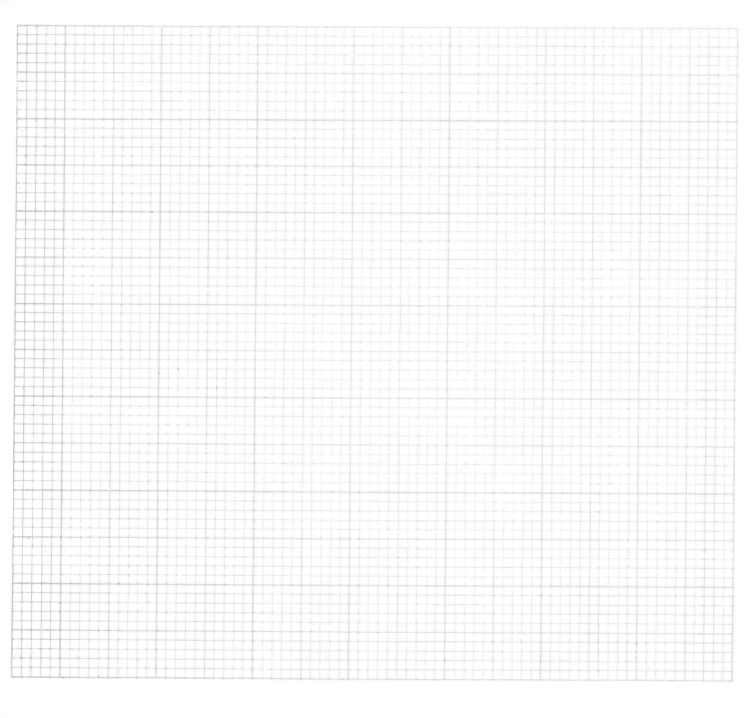

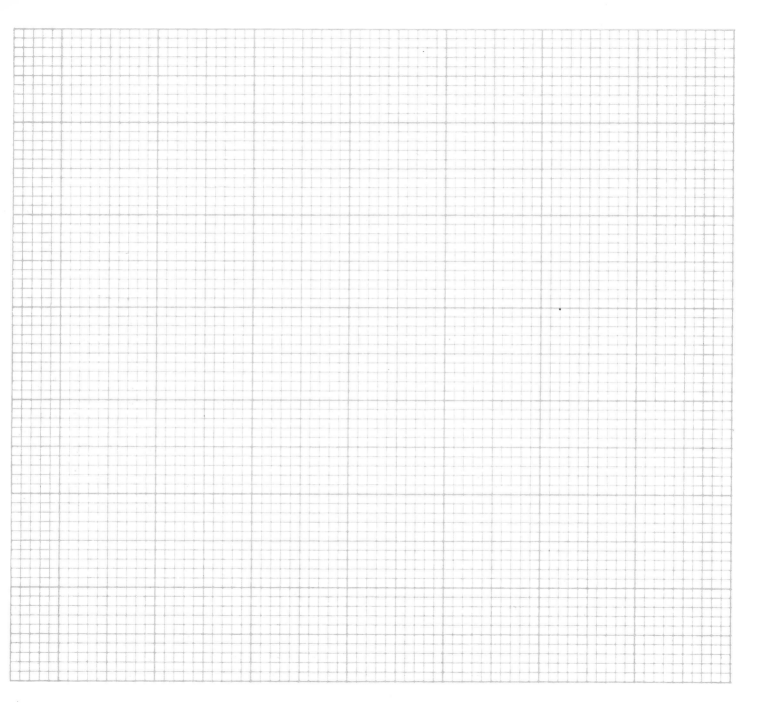

WIDE SPACING

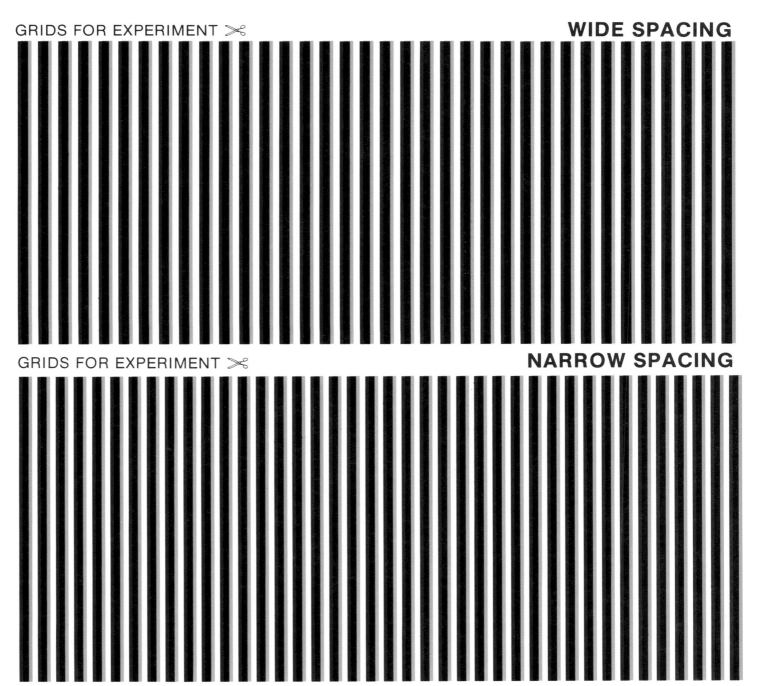

GRIDS FOR EXPERIMENT ✂

NARROW SPACING

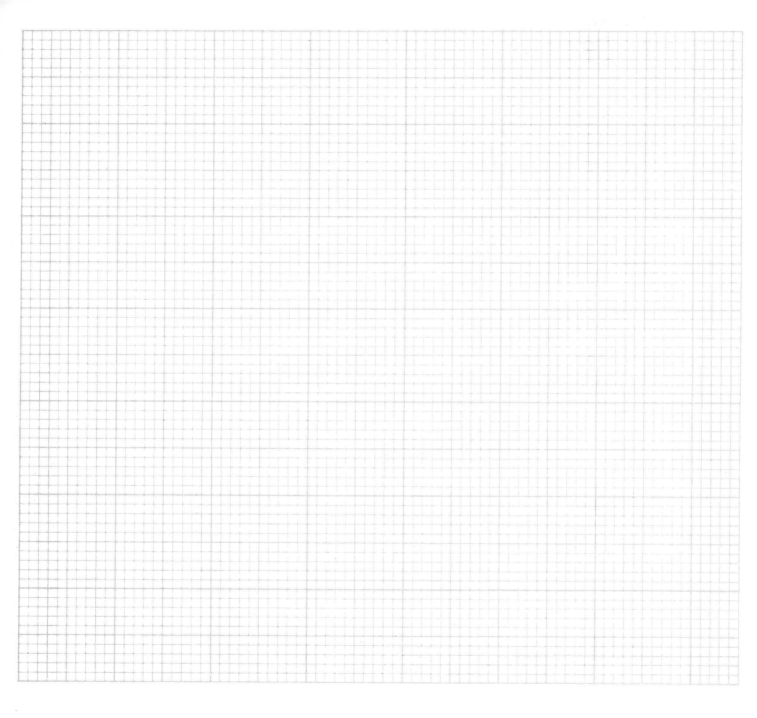

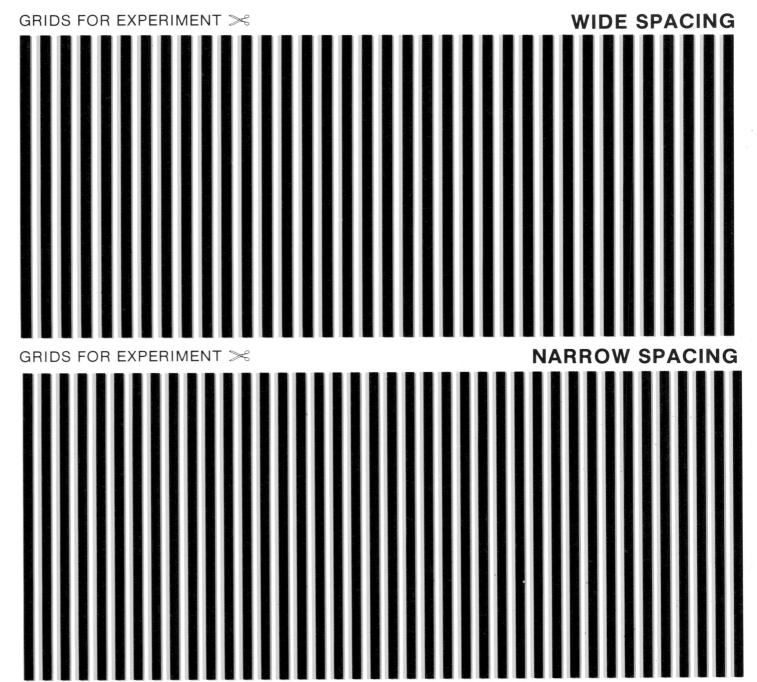

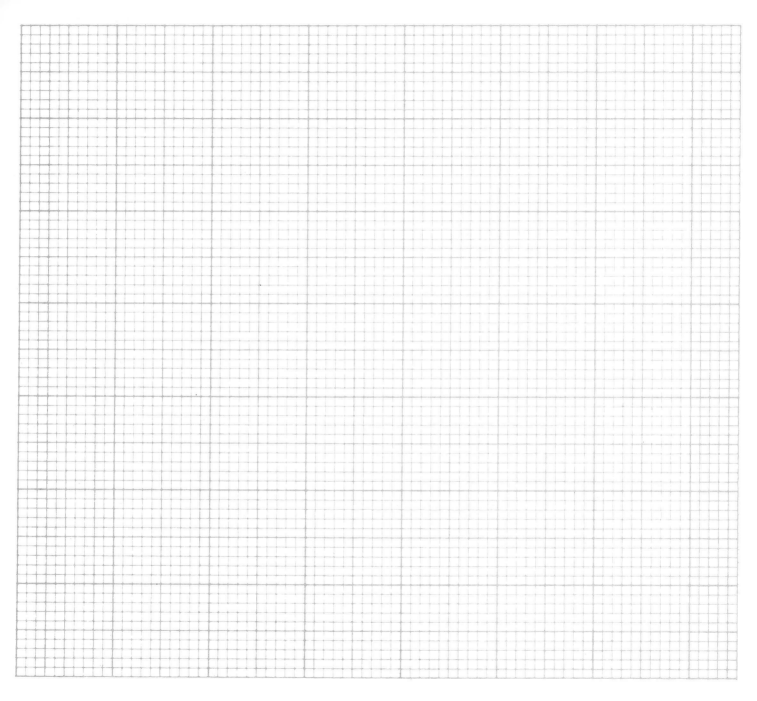

HOLLOW TRIANGLES

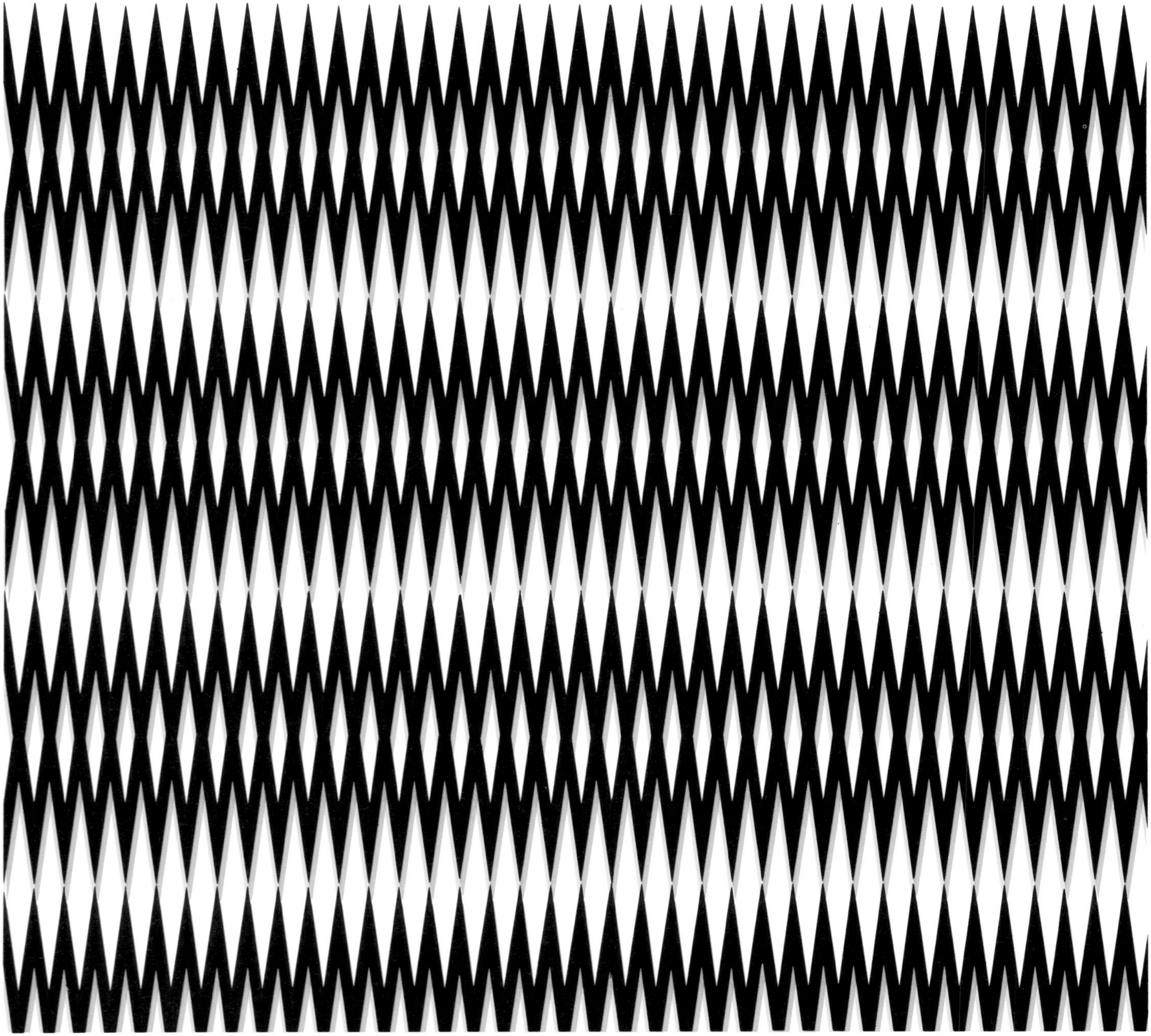

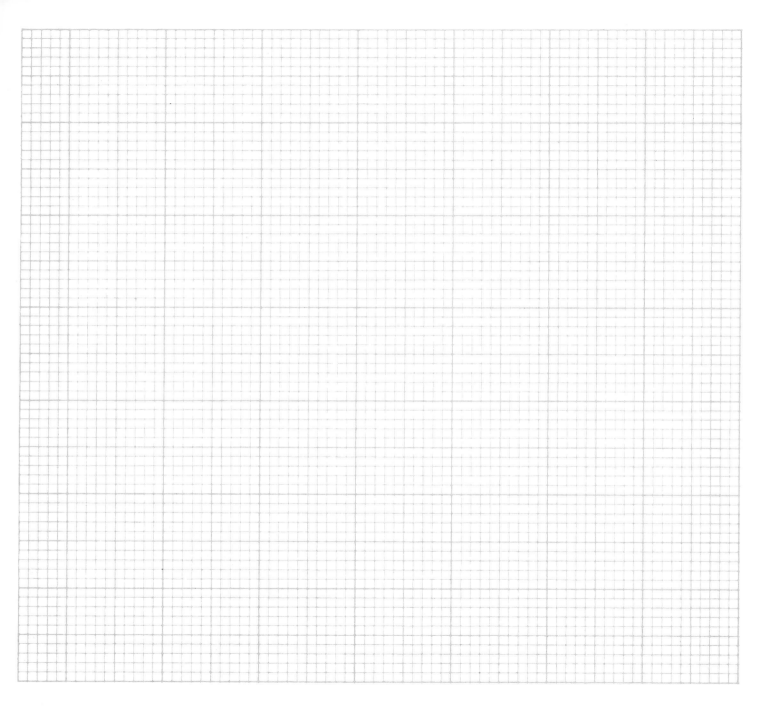

HOLLOW TRIANGLES

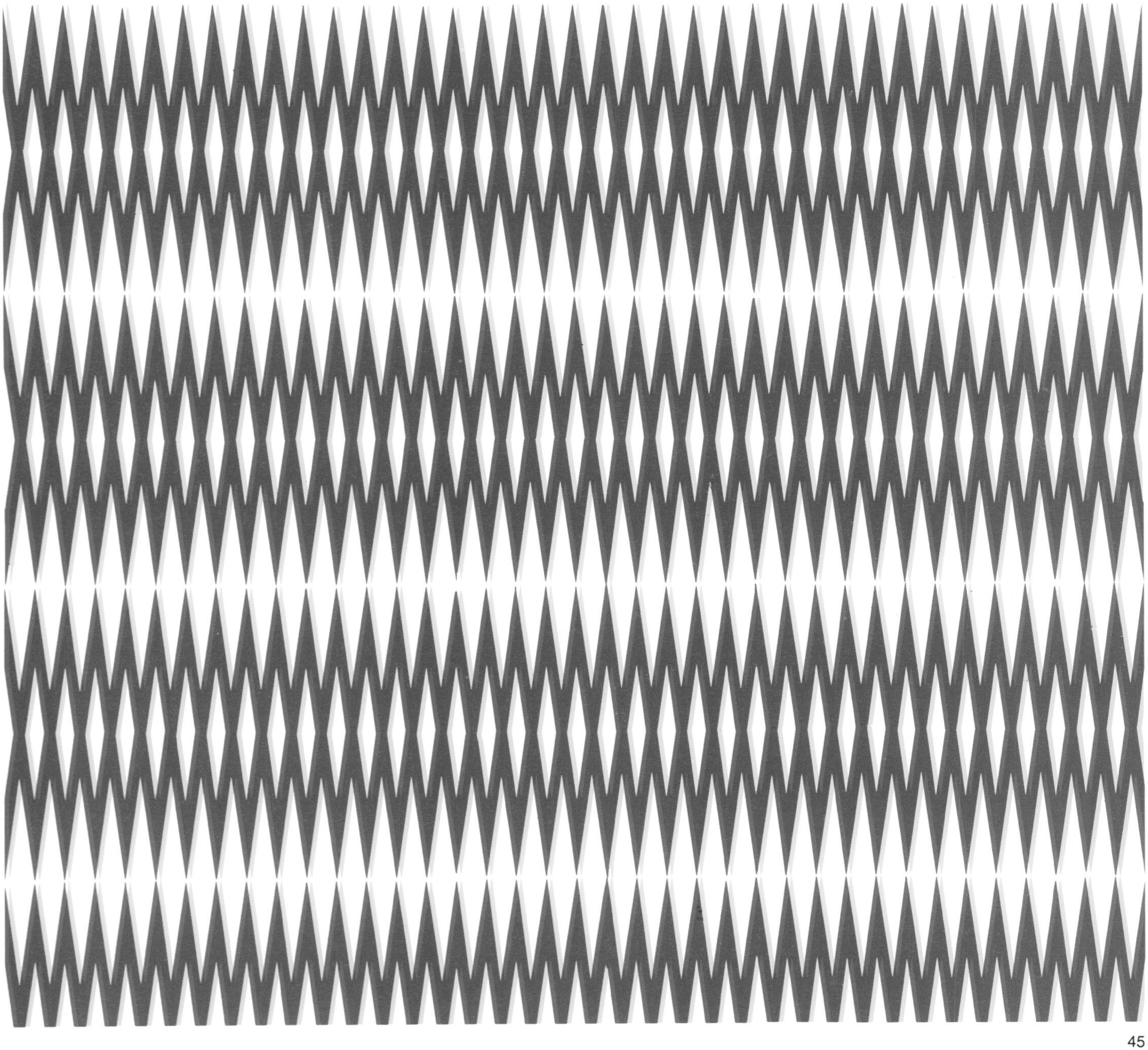

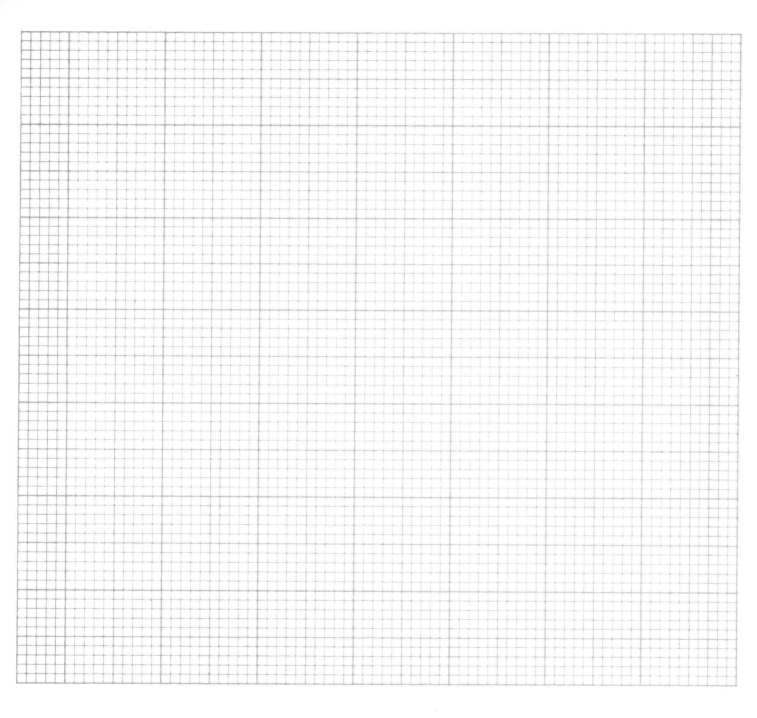

SPIKES AND ICICLES

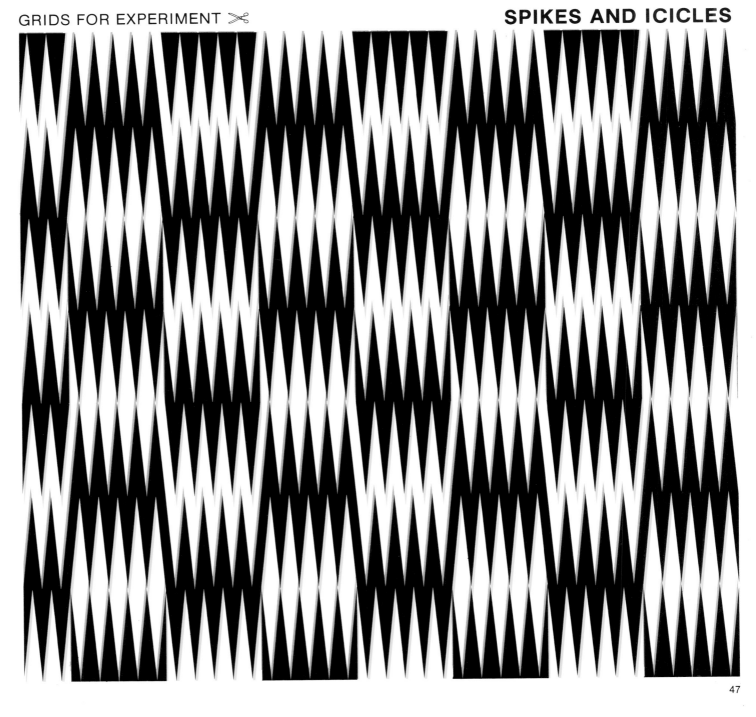

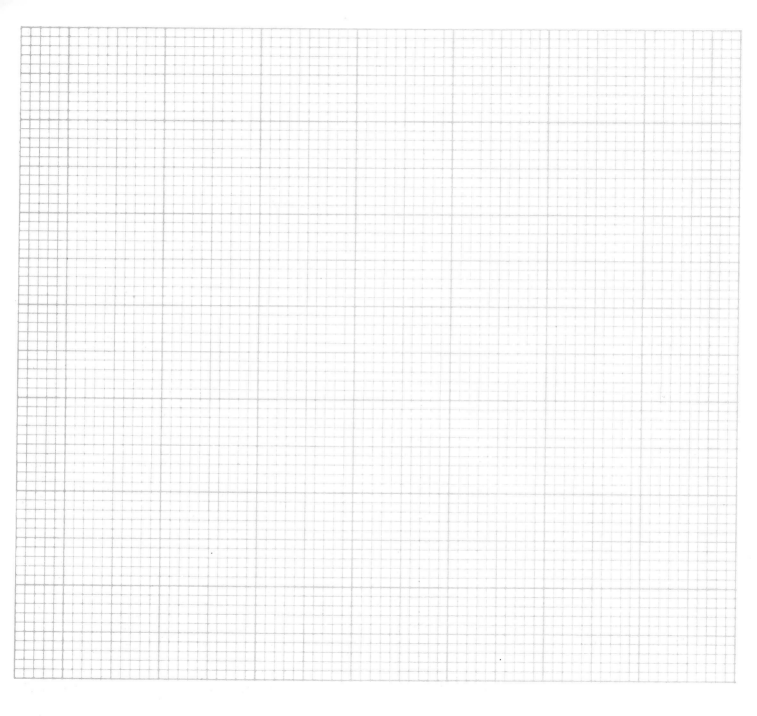

SPIKES AND ICICLES

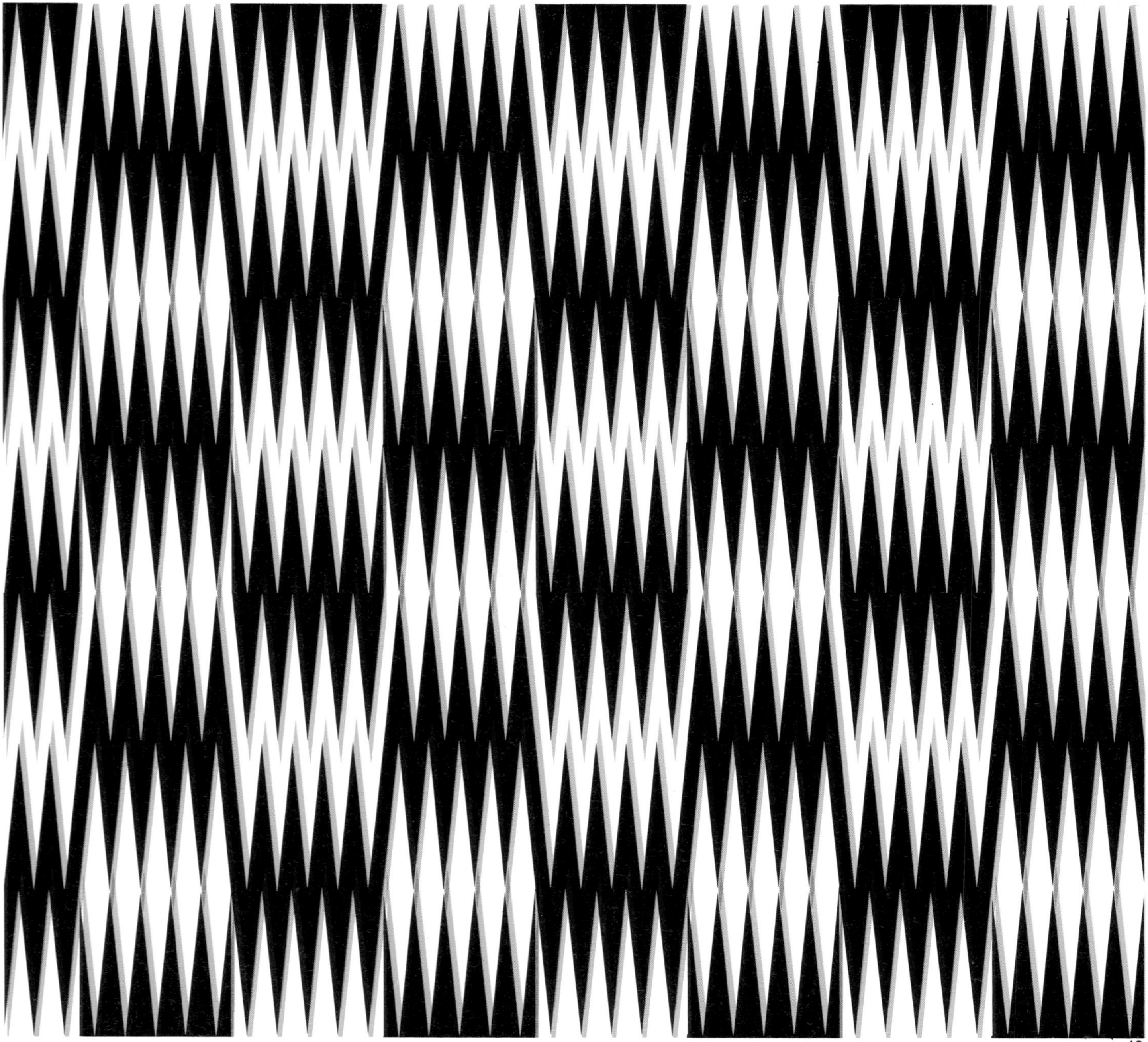

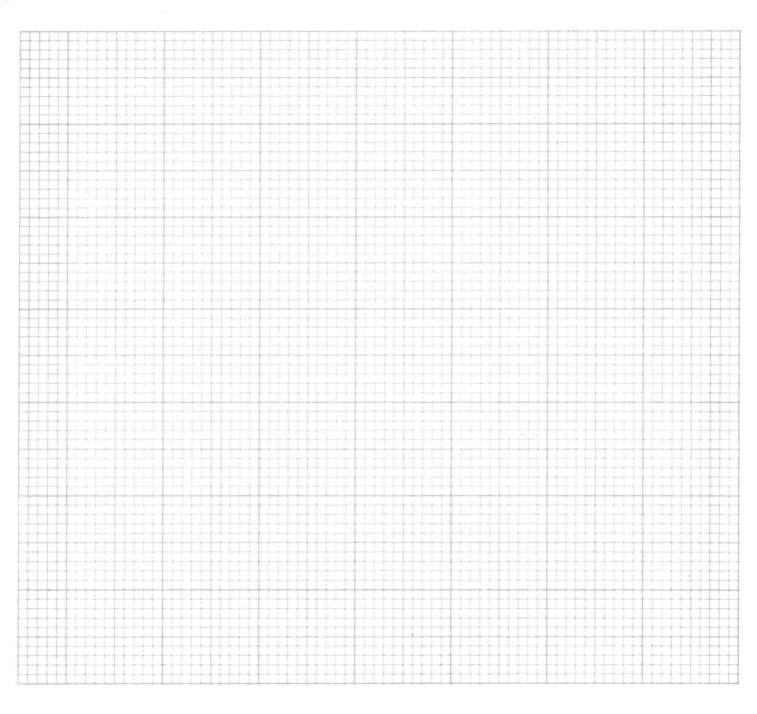

CHEVRONS

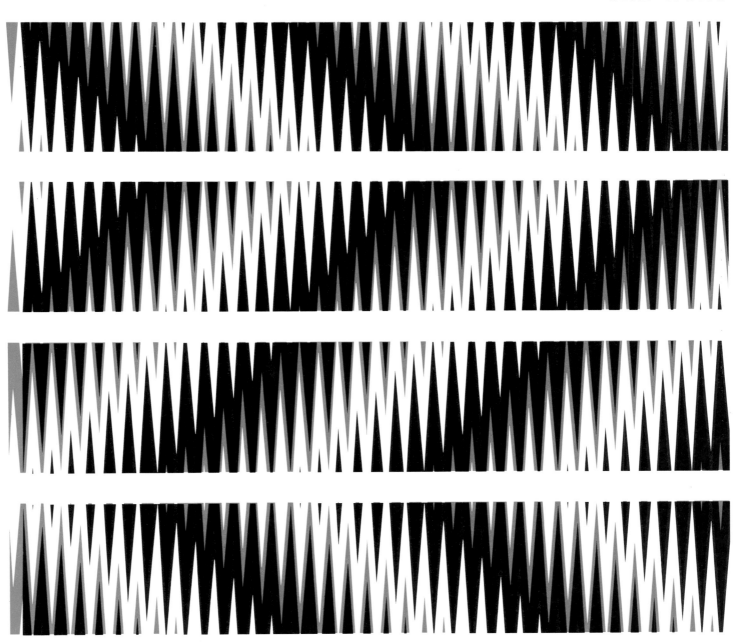

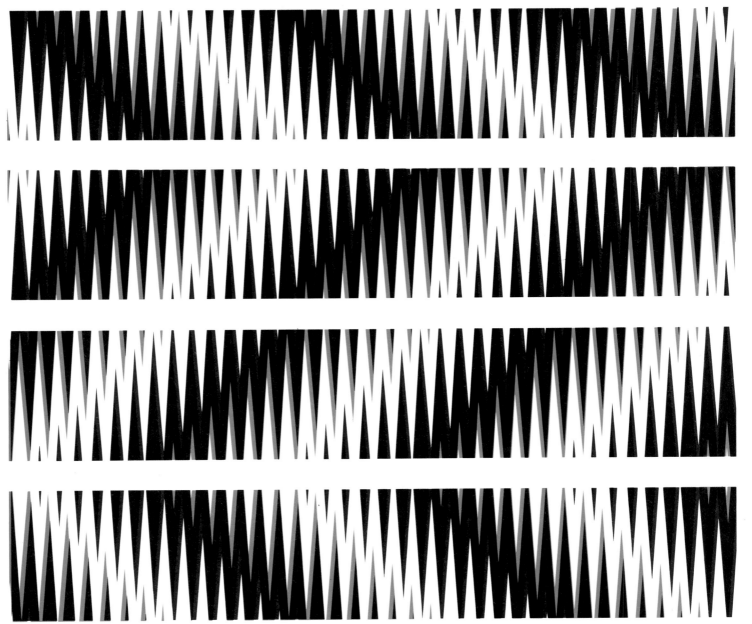

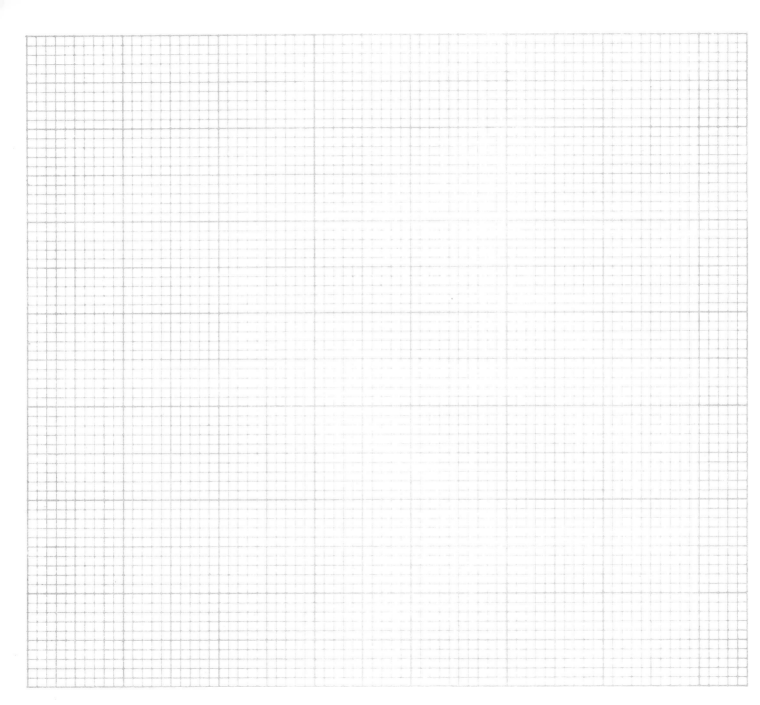

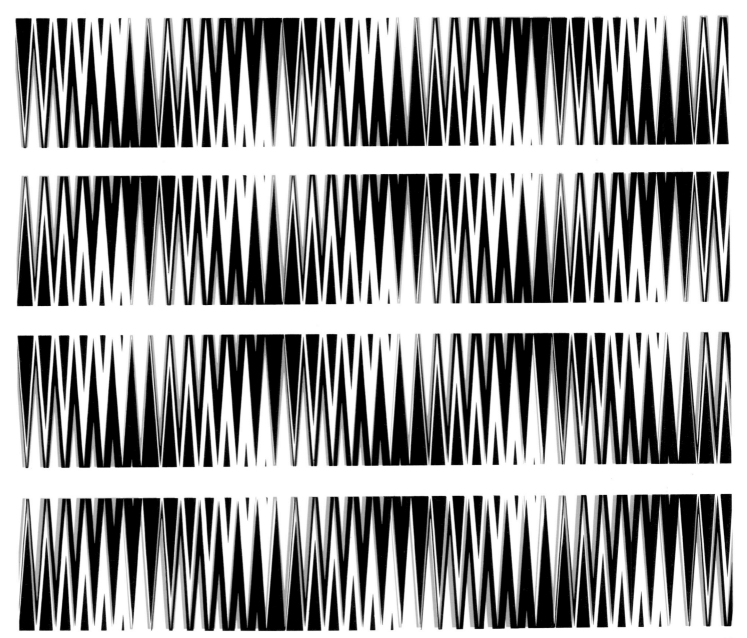

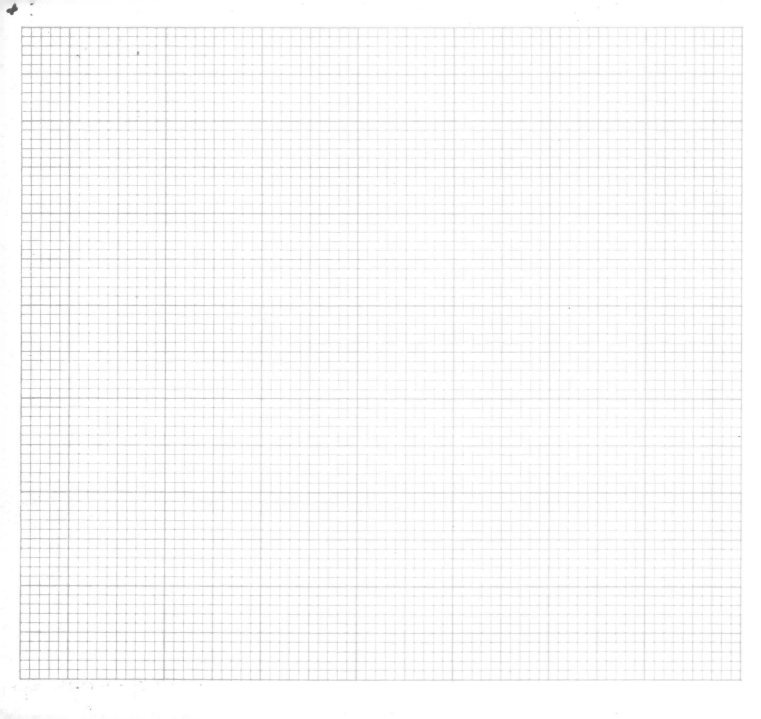